I, FLY

The Buzz About Flies and How Awesome They Are

Bridget Heos
Illustrated by Jennifer Plecas

SCHOLASTIC INC.

ISBN 978-1-338-03757-9

12 11 10 9 8 7 6 5 4 3 2 1   16 17 18 19 20 21

Printed in the U.S.A.   40

This edition first printing, January 2016

Designed by Ashley Halsey
The artist used traditional media and Photoshop to create the illustrations for this book.

To Sarah and Maddie Day
—B. H.

For Mom and Dad—
a bit of science comes through
—J. P.

Sigh.

It's always the
butterflies.
I get it.

They have such beautiful wings!

Such graceful flight!

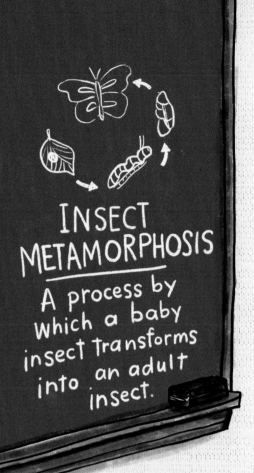

INSECT METAMORPHOSIS

A process by which a baby insect transforms into an adult insect.

Such an amazing metamorphosis!

Well, guess who else metamorphoses, can fly, and is beautiful (at least according to my mother).

Like butterflies, flies go through metamorphosis, too!

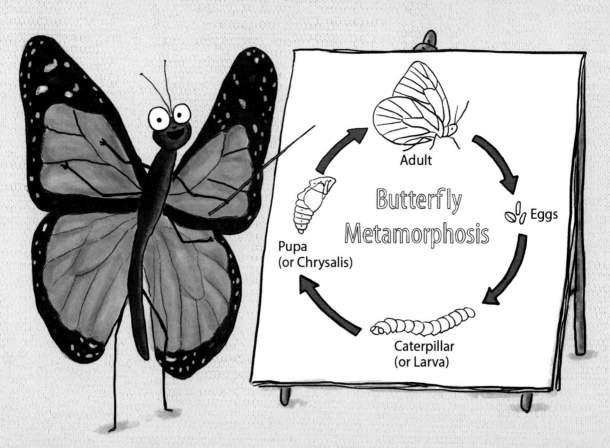

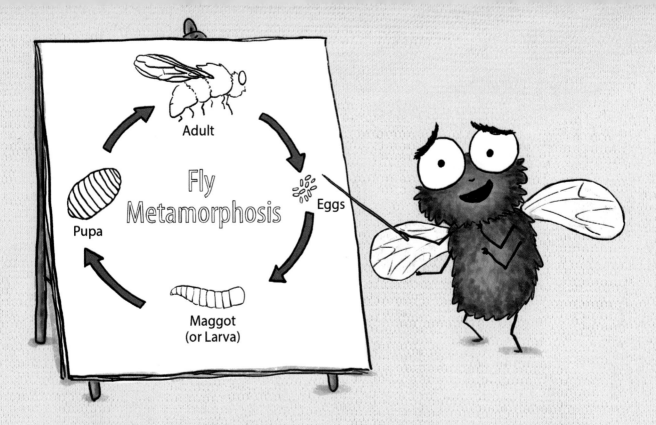

Here's how the story goes: My 500 brothers and sisters and I started out as eggs. Our mom tucked us into a warm, smelly bed of dog doo. When we hatched, we looked like short, greasy white worms. In other words, much cuter than caterpillars. Scientists called us larvae. Humans called us maggots. Our parents called us

Back in my maggot days, I ate a lot! But my siblings and I didn't eat flowers like those fancy-schmancy caterpillars. We ate poop and trash. And we still do.

Wait a second! Is that a trash can?

Yum. Rotting fruit. You don't mind if I eat
while we talk, do you?

Anyway, as maggots, we grew bigger.
We shed our skin three times.
Then we became pupae.
Inside the pupal case, things got
interesting.
We changed into flies.

I remember it like it was yesterday. I busted out of my pupal case, ate some dead meat on a bun, and then started my family.

Before I knew it, I was the father of 500 babies.

My babies grew up in ten days. Then my daughters laid about 500 eggs each. That blessed me with thousands of grandmaggots! (Or more. To be honest, I lost count.)

Sadly, my maggots and grandmaggots don't have much use for their old man. They take care of themselves— just like I did as a maggot. So now I spend most of my time flying.

I'm an amazing flier.

My wings flutter 200 times a second.
The monarch butterfly flaps its wings only
5 to 12 times per second. I scoff at that number.

Also, butterflies are annoyingly
quiet. My wings make a cool noise.

When I flap my
wings fast, I make a
high-pitched bzzzzz.

When I flap my wings slow, the
bzzzzz is low-pitched.

Maybe if your science teacher won't let you study me, your music teacher will.

And to think, I do all this with only two wings!
Those lazy butterflies have four. Even *you* could fly
with four wings, I bet. But try flying with two!

And try doing
this without

spinning

That's thanks to my halteres, little spinning things
that look like lollipops and help me keep my balance.

out

of

control.

Guess who doesn't have any.

(If you said those clumsy butterflies, you're right.)

No. We don't throw up on everything. Only solid foods.

See, we don't have any teeth, so we can't chew. I had to throw up on this apple core to turn it into a liquid. That way I could sop it up with my spongy mouth.

But if something's already a liquid, like the soup you're having for lunch, I don't throw up on it. I'll slurp that right out of the bowl.

Okay, that is true. Guilty as charged.

setae ↓

But I'm actually a really clean guy! Have you noticed that I scrub myself every time I land? It's to keep the setae (tiny hairs on my body) clean.

These hairs help me sense things, like the swoosh of air when somebody tries to swat me. But the setae can't do their job when they're cluttered with dirt and dust. Unfortunately, all that scrubbing sends bacteria flying. Sorry about that. Just keeping it clean, my friends.

Mosquitoes are flies. But they're not houseflies. They're our distant cousins. How would you feel if your distant relatives did something mean and everyone blamed you for it? Sad, right?

Well, welcome to my world.

I'm sorry. Please, don't mind my tears. It's just that my whole life—all 21 days of it—I've watched kids like you learn about butterflies. Meanwhile, I've been here all along, totally ignored.

But you can change that. Ask your teacher if you can study flies, not butterflies. We're the better species.

Listen, I made a mistake. I don't belong here in the classroom. I didn't mention it before, but I carry 1,941,000 kinds of bacteria. You think it doesn't matter that I throw up on your food? I cause 65 known human diseases. I'm filthy!

I think you should study butterflies after all, as much as it pains me to say it. Just let me out of here!

Thank you!

While I admit flies aren't great for school habitats, we really are awesome. How about a few more facts before I buzz out of here?

You don't see flies when it's cold outside. So where do new flies come from in the spring? If we lay our eggs in late fall, our larvae or pupae spend the winter deep inside whatever muck they call home. The next spring, they become flies.

If all 500 of my maggots grew up to have 500 babies of their own, that would make 250,000 new flies. Next, those 250,000 new flies could each lay 500 eggs. In a perfect world, a fly like me could have 191,010,000,000,000,000,000 (one hundred ninety-one quintillion, ten quadrillion) children and grandchildren in the course of a summer.

Unfortunately, we don't all survive. Some of us freeze on cold nights or wash away during storms.

Others are eaten by wasps, birds, bats, spiders, or dragonflies.

 SPLAT Swatters swat us.

And sometimes there isn't enough food.

You can do your part to fight fly hunger by leaving your sandwiches, ice cream cones, and candy lying around!

We're good people...
I mean insects!

Not all my relatives cause
problems, like the mosquito does.

Blowflies help police
detectives solve crimes.

The age of maggots on a dead body helps
police determine when a crime occurred.

1 DAY

4 DAYS

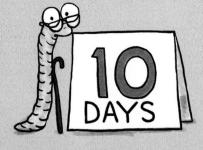

10 DAYS

And fruit flies lend a hand in science labs. Scientists like to study these fly cousins to learn why humans get sick.

Perhaps one day you'll study flies, after all!

And keep in mind that we, the houseflies, also do our part. If it weren't for our hungry maggots, the earth would be a messy place.

Glossary and Some Other Fun Words to Know

caterpillar A butterfly or moth larva. While they are popular, scientific evidence shows that they are not as cute as maggots.

environmentalist 1. A person who protects the earth's resources. 2. A muck-eating maggot.

halteres (HAL·teer·eez *or* HAL·teerz) Two thread-like organs that help flies keep their balance. They resemble lollipops. Mmm . . . lollipops.

insect metamorphosis The process by which a larva transforms into an adult insect.

larva (*pl.* larvae: LAR·vee) An offspring that is significantly different from its parent. A maggot, for instance, doesn't have much in common with a fly, except for its good looks.

maggot A type of larva that is the cute and cuddly offspring of a fly.

milkweed 1. A perennial flower with pods. 2. The plant monarch caterpillars gobble up, making pigs of themselves.

molt The process by which a larva sheds its skin, so that it can grow bigger.

petunia A popular potted flower that caterpillars rudely chew holes in.

pupa (PYU·pa; *pl.* pupae: PYU·pee) The stage during which a larva metamorphoses from maggot to fly.

 pupal case The casing in which a larva metamorphoses. A maggot uses its own skin. A butterfly caterpillar spins a chrysalis (a fancy word for a pupal case).

ptilinum (ti·LEE·num) A structure like a water balloon that pops out of a fly's head and helps it bust out of its pupal case. It disappears but leaves a cool scar.

setae (SEE·tee) Tiny hairs on insects' bodies. They help flies to sense things.

zinnia Another flower that caterpillars eat without asking.

Select Bibliography

Bicknell, Richard. "Why Do Flies and Mosquitoes Buzz?" City of Palo Alto: cityofpaloalto.org/civica/filebank/blobdload. asp?BlobID=17111 (retrieved Sept. 8, 2009).

Connor, Steven. *Fly*. London: Reaktion Books, 2006.

"Flapping Flight: A Look at Flight in Slow Motion." Annenburg Media: Journey North, 1997–2009: learner.org/jnorth/ fall2003/monarch/Update092603.html (retrieved October 19, 2009).

"Fly Information." The University of Arizona, 1997: http:// insected.arizona.edu/flyinfo.htm (retrieved October 6, 2009).

"House Flies." Penn State College of Agricultural Studies: Entomology: ento.psu.edu/extension/factsheets/house-flies (retrieved Sept. 10, 2009).

"Insect Vision: Ommatidium Structure and Function." L.L. Keeley: physioviva.com/movies/ommatidium_struc-func/index.html (retrieved October 6, 2009).

O'Toole, Christopher, Editor. *The Encyclopedia of Insects*. New York: Facts on File, 1986.

Physics Activities. "Strike a Chord: The Science of Music": http://strikeachord.questacon.edu.au/assets/strike_a_chord_physic_activities.pdf (retrieved Oct. 21, 2009).

Sanchez-Arroyo, Hussein, and John L. Capinera. "House Fly." University of Florida Institute of Food and Agricultural Sciences: entnemdept.ufl.edu/creatures/urban/flies/house_fly.htm (retrieved Oct. 6, 2009).

"Special Neurons Help Flies Sense the Wind." Insciences Organisation: insciences.org/article.php?article_id=3231 (retrieved October 6, 2009).

Experts

Thanks to the following experts for helping me
learn how awesome flies are:

Dr. Timothy Schowalter
Professor and Head of
Entomology, Louisiana
State University

Geoff Day
Entomologist and
Biology Teacher,
Eudora High School,
Eudora, Kansas

Dr. Elzie McCord
Associate Professor of
Entomology and Insect
Toxicology, New College
of Florida